MY DEDICATION

First of all, I just want to say thank you to my father god without him where would I be or what would I do it was him who brought me this far. I want to say Mommy I love you sooooo much you have inspired me to start writing since I was six and kept me strong, keeping me focus and determined that no matter what you're a fighter. I will always love you and trust me we won't struggle no more.

Thank you to my daughter's Lai'myai,Lama'jaz and Laa'jae for giving mommy the strength and energy saying mommy go,go,go you can do it, and I can't forget my big sister Ju Ju without her sisterly love and some of her time with me and saying you got all this talent sitting publish it. I love her forever no one can take her place as she walks along side with Me, My Mommy, My loving girls, My future husband and no other than our father I love u Y!

SINGLE MOTHER

By Rhonda Brignac

You left me to be a single mother

I never thought the man whom I once

knew

That I shared my most inner thoughts,

feelings and oh yea

How fast I grew to love you

You made me feel as though you we're

the only man I

Ever liked, loved and knew

Especially that day when I stepped into

womanhood and lost

My most valuable treasure

As you held me at niter when I was

happy, stressed or even sad

We planned this fairytale that momma

always had

Which was a houseman husband,

precious grandchildren?

But she also stated I think baby he

would make a wonderful dad

So scared, so anxious, so ready, so

willing to walk down the aisle

Saying I can't wait and I'll be glad

Except just when it all turned for the bad

Now momma's sad

And daddy's mad

Saying in the back of my mind

I thought this was a good thing I had

Now two babies I've had

Which we're our creations

Now I find out you had outside relations

It's cool I just wish I would have saw it

coming

Before I gave up everything

Like the finer things, which have?

Always been giving to me and being that

this was reality

While I was wasting my time living a

fantasy chasing a dream

I get tired of a typical broth who

Never pays for nothing for his kids

But when they get big

He wants to say how proud he is

Especially once they get rich and

famous

Thank you for showing me what a

Bastard is and how you are some kind

of ex-fiancée,

Liar, lover

And a stupid mothafucker

You made me stronger

I came out on top

You're in jail

Crying saying baby please I'm sorry

Can you call my mother, father, sister,

or brother?

I say I have a few words that is you're

kids no longer

Look at you as the father

And did I tell you I'm now a successful

lawyer

Who is engaged to a doctor?

So with this being said I remember one

thing

From you and that is how

"You left me to be a single mother"

STRUGGLE YOU'LL NEVER UNDERSTAND!
By Rhonda Briganic

It was a struggle you'll never understand

As I sit back and think about some of

the moments I had

Even if it was all good or even straight

up had

you can never guess

or begin the pain I went threw

But through it all I stood tall and strong

to let this flower grow from a blossom

to a lovely bloom

And I thought you were someone

who I could trust

laugh and most of

all talk to

Boy, I tell you don't know the half

Jus add it all up in you do the math

I showed the side of a mother to a

daughter

Father to a son

But just not the daughter who would be

the hustling one

How you think it wasn't all you

or them it was I

Who put the food on those plates

going through strange change

with my love ones to blame

taking love from your father and putting

it to the side

To me look in my eyes, see my tears

just know that you lied

And every day for the past 13 years

in my heart

Hell yes truly thru the blood in my heart I

cry

not leaving far behind a mother

Who at times her child thinks my mother

is not mines

as she's telling me I'm her baby

baby , the torture you put me through

even trying to please you

Just wasn't good enough for you

I hope she gets it together girl for the

love of you

and you got kids right boo

she said girl 4 beautiful ones too!

Momma didn't even know that you was

a dancer by night

And school girl who you never dreamed

would do this by day

It was a struggle you'll never understand

AIN"T NONE EVER LIKE ME!
By Rhonda Brignac

Ain't none ever like me

With the lips so soft, touch

Tender caresses from me got you

yearning to fill all this and much

yet still in all I make you blush

Fancy restaurants, expensive dining

with your imagination picturing me

winding

My sexiness carries you threw

Curvy, thick, silky hips will definitely do

The chocolate I say that melts

in your mouth not in your hands

Baby you know I have a high supply and
demand

Softness of my hands rubbing and
rubbing

To warm your body with lots of loving
boos

Classy, sassy, and a bit nasty but with a
one and only

See now look girl don't be getting all
horny

With all intents to take over

Your body where we've been

And you to say baby oh this is where I
went

The thought to yourself to think so
sexual

Just not letting your face catch a bright
glow

Cause then everybody gone know

Baby its okay to gloat

You know that's was your dream

For me to make you a part of my
mommy team

I will then love you without a doubt I will
decide

To make you and I official

But only if you're worth it

I give this honor baby only if you
deserve it

The sky is the limit for you boy

Are you willing to act like my man?

After waiting to see

Asking now is the time let's do this

officially

So if you missed out

One thing she can say is

"Ain't none ever like me"

3-5-08 10:21 p.m.

A
letter to my unborn child

Dear Baby Boy or Baby Girl mommie is going through a lot of emotions

 right now due to a lot of undisclosed reasons only mommy knows and

will explain it all to you as time goes on and you get older I can't wait

until you are born you have a lot of people waiting on you to come out

like grandma, mommy, yai yai, majaz oh yeah baby those are you're

big sister's they are so excited to see you they always are kissing my

stomach and hugging all on me because they are so anxious, baby grandpa don't even know about you yet because I know he'll just give

me this big lecture about you but oh well ne way he'll get over it and

you're so called daddy is waiting as well and we're not together but I will

explain it later to you as well it's some niggas in the world excuse my

expression baby but you'll never turn out to be like this I promise that

I am going to make sure of that because I don't know where you're

daddy got his up being from but he should have left it there because

that is why me and him isn't together because he is a big hoe and

that is something mommy have never dealt with never have and never will. I didn't put ne periods inside of this letter that I'm writing to you and

guess what i seen you a few days ago and you were soooo tiny, but

I know that soon you're gonna stretch out and you also have some

other people who are waiting on you mommie is waiting patiently and

Poo Poo u haven't met her yet but she is very special to me she has

been a part of our lives for six years she will be one of the people you

see when you come out she will be around besides that stale ass

daddy of yours she'll be around more then he will ever be but I love

u sooooooooo much and I will see u in October which is mommy

birthday month and I am signing off.

My Journey of Finger-painting

Rhonda Brignac

What was most significant for me about this experience?

What was most significant for me from this experience was I actually felt like my four

Year old little girl playing in the finger-paint, learning that it's fun to play, explore, learn

and interesting. Before doing this I have never come close to playing in any paint

period, so when I got the chance to experience playing in this paint I was bored, but

then I thought and put myself in my daughter's shoes, so then I understood and it

became fun to do.

Did this experience engage you in exploration, experimentation and /or discovery?

Yes this experience did engage me

exploration, experimentation and

discovery they all are self-explanatory,

for me exploration is about exploring

different objects, books, paints etc.

allowing yourself to just let your

imagination run free, experimentation is

just trying fun things also not so fun

things and discovery is just discovering

something a child may have never

thought it would be possible to do. I

think by doing this it helps to relieve

stress and allow you to free your mind I

think we should be able to listen to our

own music also

but I guess this is the kind of music that

maybe

soothing for other's I personally like

meaningful music.

Dealing with love
By Rhonda Brignac

Each and every day I'm faced with a

problem

Always trying to come up with a way to

solve them

Yet I'm always left hurting

In a situation don't know which way to

turn

To me only my feelings are fucked up

Soon to be left, heart cut up

Why do I trap myself with emotion

Out here is like seeing my happiness

rolling coasting

Hay but who am I

Is it all just a lie

Should I just let it go and let it die

Or just make you cry

It's my hands that you got tied

For once in life can we

follow the proper chain of command

Do we have to run every time we think

our lives

our ruined

I just want you to sit back, pay attention

and take notes

Figuring that you would continue to let

us grow

Anyway I guess what do I know

I knew once I became a woman

It would be rough for me to be

"Dealing with love"

What is love
By Rhonda Brignac

Most people say that they know what

love means but really don't

too me I think it's just the lust that you

actually want

or was this some type of thing in which

you thought of

At times sitting and concentrating on

how it could be something

Not really wanting to believe that I'm

holding onto a dream hay it was once a

reality

but when I think back that wasn't me

It was you setting me up for failure

Could I classify you as a liar maybe

better yet a cheater or should I say a

 deceiver

Ok maybe not literally but at heart

Though I must admit you had that part

I always knew what it meant I'm just not

as sure that you knew

that i was and am still a blessing to all in

this world

hmm might I add definitely sent from up

above

Just asking do you know

What is love

Y I ask U
By Rhonda Brignac

Everytime u turn around it's always a

excuse

But I understand that's what your use to

and that's what people do

Did it cross your mind u might ask me

for a favor or question

why should I give you the time to sit an

converse with me for any reason

You remember yea it was you ha,ha,ha

I tricked you

Now look at u, is that a sour face I see

boo

Ooh no know not you

It jus slip my mind you are better than

me

This is just why I play you the way you

need to be

The last thing I did wanna mention

I just won that big check for twenty-five

thousand Whoo hoo

And you wanna know don't you in life I'm
just wondering

"Y I ask U"